Isle of Wight
FERRIES

John Hendy

C000260970

PO Box 33, Ramsey,
Isle of Man, IM99 4LP

Tel: +44 (0) 1834 898445
Fax: +44 (0) 1834 898449

www.wightlink.co.uk

St Helen

ST. HELEN

Introduction

On 7th November 1990 the new brand name and livery of Wightlink were unveiled when the Fishbourne ferry *St. Faith*, Lymington's *Caedmon* and the Portsmouth - Ryde catamaran *Our Lady Pamela* were all paraded before the press in Spithead.

Five years later, in June 1995, Michael Aiken led the management buy-in of Wightlink for £107.5 million backed by the Royal Bank of Scotland and venture capital company CinVen. This caused the company become totally independent and private for the first time in its history. In October 2001 the management team brought out CinVen's interest to take a majority shareholding in the company.

Over five million passengers and well over one million cars in addition to 160,000 coach and freight units each year presently travel with Wightlink generating a revenue of some £46 million.

Of the three routes, the youngest is also the busiest and traffic growth on the Portsmouth - Fishbourne route has been phenomenal. Fishbourne is truly the 'Gateway to the Isle of Wight.'

The quieter western Solent link from Lymington to Yarmouth is totally different in character and is, in many ways, the back door to the Isle of Wight. Its ships are regularly capacity constrained during the summer months and Wightlink are assessing the situation with regard to extra tonnage on the route.

The traditional service is the passenger crossing from Portsmouth Harbour to Ryde Pier Head which is today operated by Wightlink's fleet of FastCats. Of all the routes, this has seen the greatest change from coal-fired wooden paddle steamers to modern high-speed catamarans driven by waterjets.

This publication explains how the three services grew and developed to enable Wightlink to become the major force that we see today. At the beginning of a new century, the island's number one operator can be justly proud of its past achievements and is able to look to the future with a degree of well-earned confidence.

John Hendy
johnfhendy@hotmail.com
January 2002

Foreword

by Michael Aiken, Chief Executive, Wightlink Ltd.

I was delighted to be asked to write the foreword to yet another excellent book researched, created and produced by John Hendy. His fascination with, and research into, the background and history of Great Britain's seaways and shipping companies enables the reader to have a unique insight into our Island's nautical heritage.

In the case of this book he has recorded the history and events of Wightlink, the UK's largest independent ferry operator. Our role in life has always been to provide the essential sea 'lifelines' between the Isle of Wight and the mainland on our three short sea routes across the Solent, 24 hours a day, 365 days a year and currently with a fleet of twelve vessels.

I am sure that you will enjoy John Hendy's historical account.

PORTSMOUTH - FISHBOURNE
The Premier Link

Although the Fishbourne route is historically the youngest of all the links to the Isle of Wight, it is today by far the busiest of them and justly deserves its position of the number one 'Gateway to the Island.'

For many years, the main entry into the island for goods, livestock and, later, motor cars was at George Street slipway, to the east of Ryde Pier. It was far from ideal and operational problems beset it at low water when the sea retreated almost as far as the pierhead. What was required was a sheltered deep water berth in

Loading the horse-boats at Broad Street slipway. In the background is Portsmouth Harbour Station. (Eric Payne collection)

CONVEYANCE OF MOTOR VEHICLES (Which can be run on and off Boats with own power), Horses, Carriages, Vans, Cattle, etc.; TO & FROM THE ISLE OF WIGHT every Week Day, by powerful Steam Tug and Tow Boats.
(Weather and other circumstances permitting)

From PORTSMOUTH (Broad St. Slipway) for RYDE

About TWO HOURS before High Water.

From RYDE (George St. Slipway) for PORTSMOUTH

About HALF-AN-HOUR before High Water.

Information as to actual times of departure from Portsmouth and Ryde may be obtained at the Marine Superintendent's Offices, 102 Broad Street, Portsmouth (Tel. 4655), Portsmouth Harbour Pier (Tel. 6077), or from the Station Master, Ryde (Tel. 247).

Senders or Owners of Horses, Carriages, Motor Cars, Live Stock, etc., by Tow Boat, take upon themselves all risk of Conveyance, and of loading or unloading, as the Companies will not be answerable for accidents or damage done to any property, live stock, etc. All traffic must be at the place of embarkation half-an-hour before time of sailing, and in charge of Senders' or Owners' Servants who must accompany it.

the area of Ryde which would enable this specialist traffic to be handled at all states of the tide.

Two miles west of Ryde is Wootton Creek and it was here that the Southern Railway purchased some 2 acres of ground and prepared for their improved service early in 1925.

The work involved dredging a deep water channel to give a depth of 8 ft. at low spring tides. Four dolphins were erected at the entrance to the creek to indicate the designed course and a lay-by basin some 200 ft. square was also prepared with mooring for the tugs and boats engaged in the towing.

On shore, the work started on 10th March 1925 and a new road was constructed to meet the end of Fishbourne Lane. New offices and waiting rooms, a car-parking space with a lock-up garage, standings for 15 cows, pens for 100 pigs and 6 boars, a house for the clerk in charge and a public telephone for the convenience of the public were all installed.

The work of deepening the channel meanwhile was delayed as the soft mud kept falling back into the dredged area and the opening, which had been planned for August, was therefore delayed.

In the event, the transfer took place on Monday 15th March 1926 giving a crossing time of rather longer than the old route. The tow-boats would be grounded on a specially constructed slipway and large planks, or loading boards, would be laid-out to ease the angle between boat and shore. Although the tugs pulled three tow-boats at one time, the slip was only large enough to accommodate one and it took about 2 minutes to load each car. To start with, two round trips each day were given although at peak times this was

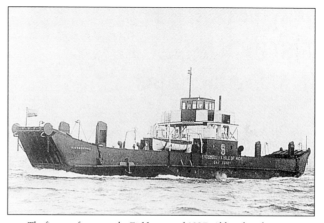

*The first car ferry was the **Fishbourne** of 1927. Although rather primitive when compared with today's ships, she represented a tremendous advance on the tow-boats that she replaced. (George Cook collection)*

increased. Motor cars carried in 1923 had numbered 1,168, in 1924 this had risen to 1,356 while in 1925, 1,718 had been shipped. Fares in the new service remained the same as before e.g. 22/- (£1.10) single for a car of between 10 -14 ft. in length.

Although most motorists remained in their cars (there was no room for them to stretch their legs on the tow-boats which only held three cars each), some would continue to travel over in the steamer from Ryde and find their way to Fishbourne to reclaim their vehicles. The tow-boats offered nothing by way of protection and were frequently covered in spray and there was always the chance that your car might share a crossing with frightened

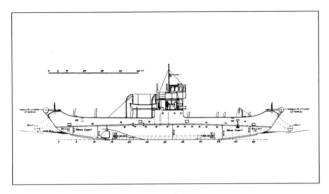

Wootton (1928)

Fishbourne (1961)

livestock which would show their displeasure of the experience in nature's own special way. Needless to say, the Southern's new service was for the strong of heart and the hardy of nose.

DRIVE ON

With the improved route hardly able to cope, the Southern Railway entered into negotiations with Messrs. Denny of Dumbarton for the building of a special vessel. Much detail had to be discussed - should the new craft be double-ended, how should it be propelled, should there be facilities for the passengers?

The result was a punt-like, self-propelled ferry of some 131 ft in length with a beam of 25 ft. It was supplied with four screws and four rudders, given a ladies' and a gentlemen's saloon and offered the travelling motorists light refreshments on the passage. As many

*The **Hilsea** of 1930 off Broad Street slip and waiting for the old Portsmouth - Gosport floating bridge to cross the harbour entrance.*

*In July 1972, the **Camber Queen** loads for Portsmouth. (John Hendy collection)*

as 16 cars could be shipped at one time.

The revolutionary *Fishbourne* cost £13,254 to build and was launched on 21st June 1927. She completed a successful trial trip from Southampton to Fishbourne on 13th August and came into service ten days later. Two return crossings were given each day, the passage being 55 minutes at 8 knots. Instead of loading planks linking boat with shore, the new *Fishbourne* was fitted with a fold-down bow which was manually operated. This was later fitted with

an electric winch to speed up matters but the ramp itself could take loads of up to 8 tons. Early problems over the operation of the ship as a double-ender were solved by making her run bow-first in both directions and while she was off service, the old tow boat service, which had been retained for the shipment of cattle, was reinstated. Her success saw the second vessel, the *Wootton*, on order which was fitted with larger ramps and was able to take more motor cars. An increase in the electrical power available was made

*The **Cuthred** entered service in 1969 and was the first of the third generation of Isle of Wight car ferries having a passenger deck across the top of the car deck. She was withdrawn from service at the end of the 1986 season. (John Hendy collection)*

Lymington - Yarmouth crossing.

By the late fifties the three old ferries were becoming increasingly outdated, unable to cope with the traffic on offer or with the schedules demanded.

Two new larger and faster ferries were ordered from Philip & Son of Dartmouth and were launched on 15th March and 13th April 1961 being named *Fishbourne* and *Camber Queen* respectively. The second ship was originally to have been named *Wootton* but a mainland name was chosen instead. As the ferries ran from a dock known as the Camber, the choice of name at least kept people happy on both sides of the Solent.

In order to free their names for the new ships, the first *Fishbourne* and *Wootton* were given the suffix II. The premier craft was replaced on service on 7th July when the new *Fishbourne*

and the saloons were larger - all after gaining the initial experience with the prototype. The *Wootton* was delivered at Portsmouth in June 1928 and a virtual sister, the *Hilsea*, appeared on station two years later.

In 1929, the cars carried on the Fishbourne route had increased to almost 13,000 and busy summer Saturdays saw as many as fifteen trips being offered.

On the outbreak of war, one vessel was kept on station while the other two found limited employment towards the war effort. More importantly, the *Fishbourne* and the *Wootton* crossed the Channel to assist in the evacuation of Dunkirk although their use was negligible. Later in the war they both saw service on the

*In September 1978, the Dundee-built **Caedmon** is seen on passage to Fishbourne and running into a south-westerly gale. (John Hendy)*

*During 1983, the two 1961 sisters completed their final seasons on the passage. Here is the **Fishbourne** off Gilkicker Point, seen from the bridge of the new **St. Catherine**. (John Hendy)*

entered service but two days later was called out of retirement when she went off service with ramp problems. The *Wootton II* and the *Hilsea* finished in September and October after the *Camber Queen* had entered service on 29th August.

Both new ships were similar in design to the western Solent's *Freshwater* (1959) although as the Fishbourne route did not carry foot passengers, accommodation was provided for only 168 passengers and 34 cars. The ships were fitted with Voith Schneider propellers, a standard fixture with one exception on all the car ferries since their introduction in the western Solent ferry *Lymington* of 1938. Their speed of 10.5 knots allowed them to accomplish the crossing in about 35 minutes but such was the growth of traffic that they were soon hard-pressed to cope during the summer peaks.

It was not only the vessels which presented a new image and a general revamp of the Portsmouth - Fishbourne route. Wider slipways were built on both sides of the Solent and terminal buildings were constructed adjacent to the latest Camber berth at Portsmouth. In addition, the modern Portsmouth slip eased traffic congestion in Broad Street as the terminal was provided with its own car park and as it cleared the entrance to the Camber Docks, it no longer obstructed other shipping movements. Likewise, at Fishbourne the new slip was at right angles to the original one allowing easier access from the approach channel as it faced the sea and not Wootton Creek. A large car park was constructed too as part of the £1 million reorganisation.

Not only did the twin ships generate the usual motor car traffic, which tended to be holiday-based and therefore of a seasonal nature, but commercial vehicle traffic began to build-up too. With this in mind, a new £275,000 vehicle ferry was ordered from the Richards' yard at Lowestoft for entry into service in June 1969. This was the *Cuthred* - the first of the third generation of Isle of Wight car ferries. She duly arrived at Portsmouth on 27th June and completed her maiden voyage on the following day.

COMMERCIAL TRAFFIC

The *Cuthred* was quite different from anything previously seen, with her passenger accommodation taken right across the vehicle deck and offering far more in the way of comfort and facilities. Inside seats were available for 357 of her 400 passengers although this included 178 seats in the lower lounges, which were functional to say the least.

The new ship's name was the first of the Isle of Wight ships to receive that of a character associated with the period of English

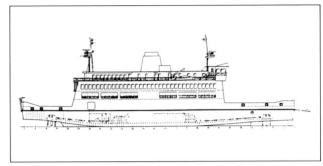

St. Catherine (1983)

history known as the Dark Ages - Cuthred being the King of Wessex between 740 - 754. This naming policy was in use during the 1970's but was later discontinued in favour of 'Saint' names.

The *Cuthred's* great drawback was that she was hopelessly under-powered and this problem was to blight her years in service with the company. However, on Christmas Day 1969 and again in 1970, she called at Ryde Pier en-route route from Portsmouth to Fishbourne which fired much speculation as to the future of the Ryde service once the three diesel ferries passed on. It seemed almost certain that Ryde would become a regular stopping place for the Fishbourne ships which would also call at Portsmouth Harbour Pier.

During early 1970, the Lymington ferry *Freshwater* appeared on the Fishbourne link just as the *Camber Queen* had deputised in the western Solent the previous October. These trials proved to be very useful as on 13th February 1970, the *Camber Queen* grounded

*The **St. Catherine** approaches Fishbourne during her first season. (John Hendy)* on a falling tide at Fishbourne after discharging her cars from the 19.00 from Portsmouth. She was not refloated until 04.00 the next morning and in the meantime, the 21.00 service to the island saw the *Fishbourne* crossing from Portsmouth to Yarmouth.

A fourth ship for Portsmouth was launched from Robb Caledon's yard at Dundee on 3rd May 1973. This was the *Caedmon*, the first of a trio of ships (the other two for Lymington) costing £1.8 million. With a capacity for 750 passengers and 52 cars, the *Caedmon* was in every way an improved *Cuthred*. She arrived at Portsmouth on 22nd July and ran her maiden voyage five days later.

Capacity problems at Portsmouth's Broad Street terminal were

Cochrane's of Selby launched the **St. Faith** *on 28th February 1990, the River Ouse not being wide enough to allow a traditional entry into the water. (John Hendy collection)*

solved by the purchase of the redundant Gunwharf site at which coal for the city's closed power station was offloaded. A £2 million loan was arranged for its purchase, the area was cleared and a brand new terminal with massive car-parking space was duly opened on 21st February 1982. The old slipway method of loading was replaced by use of a linkspan - a bridge across which vehicles drive between ship and shore. This was essential as by this time it was known that one, possibly two, fourth-generation vehicle ferries would soon replace the 1961 twins.

Early in September 1981, Sealink had also unveiled plans for a similar expansion at Fishbourne but there was much opposition to

An early morning view of the **Cuthred** *as she leaves the lay-by berths to take up service in August 1985. (John Hendy)*

*The second 'Saint' was the **St. Helen** which is seen shortly after leaving Portsmouth on a blustery Saturday morning in September 1994. (John Hendy)*

this by the local residents. However, work started in late August 1982 and was completed in June the following year.

The first of the two new ferries was the £5 million *St. Catherine*. She was launched at the Leith yard of Henry Robb on 30th March 1983, arrived at Portsmouth for trials on 24th June and entered service on 3rd July. The fourth-generation of car ferry quite outshone all others. With a passenger capacity for as many as 1,000, these Fishbourne ferries carried 142 cars. For the first time ever, passengers were actually asked to vacate their vehicles during the passage and from the ample and spacious accommodation high above the vehicle decks, they could gaze at the Solent through large panoramic windows, partake of the salt-sea air from the spacious open deck or enjoy a light snack or perhaps even something a little stronger from the well-stocked refreshment bar.

*Steam meets diesel at Fishbourne in September 1999. The Bluebell Railway's E4 class locomotive No. 473 'Birch Grove' is driven on board the **St. Faith** after attending the Isle of Wight Steam Railway's annual 'Steam Extravaganza.' (Andrew Cooke)*

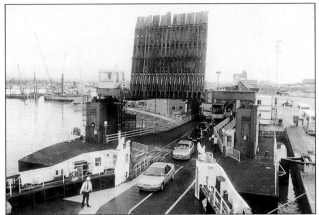

*Cars driving on board the **St. Helen** at Portsmouth's Continental Ferry Port when, on 8th September 1999, the berth at Wightlink's Gunwharf Terminal was closed for repairs. As a result of this she unusually berthed stern-in at Fishbourne. (both Andrew Cooke)*

With a gross tonnage of 2,036, the 'Catherine' was the largest Isle of Wight car ferry ever and measures 250 ft. by 55 ft. The vessel was a whole new concept in island travel and unlike any of the previous car ferries she boasted a 'proper' bow and stern and was not double ended as were the earlier generations.

Triple-screwed with three 6-cylinder Harland & Wolff M.A.N. engines, each developing 900 b.h.p. maximum speed is about 13.5 knots although only about 85% of the power is used and a service speed of 11.5 knots is operated. The main vehicle deck accommodates 88 cars while the mezzanine deck holds a further

*This view of the **St. Helen** swinging off Fishbourne clearly shows her forward Voith-Schneider propeller at work. The original quartet of 'Saint' class ships were tailor made for the route after over fifty years' experience. Since entering service these fast and efficient vessels have gained a reputation second to none. (John Hendy)*

54. With this deck raised, 24 commercial vehicles can be carried. The *Fishbourne* was retired upon the *St. Catherine's* entry into service although in early September, when the *Caedmon* went off service for 48 hours, she was brought back - the 1961 sisters (34 cars and 168 passengers) presenting a stark contrast to the new giant.

The second new ship, the *St. Helen* was launched at Leith on 15th September. She arrived at Portsmouth on 24th November and entered service four days later. Both new ships had been finished with the blue hull of the nationalised railway company, whose subsidiary Sealink U.K. Ltd. operated all British Rail's ships, but in readiness for privatisation, the double-arrow logo of British Rail was not applied to their red funnels. A new livery was introduced during the following spring and in July 1984, Sealink was privatised for £66 million -'British Ferries' being added to the name thereafter.

Whilst the *Camber Queen* was soon sold and sailed to Portugal to continue her career, the *Fishbourne* was sold to Pound's scrap yard at Tipnor, north Portsmouth, before her sale to Cyprus. Alas, she did not last long, being swamped at her moorings by a gale.

The *St. Helen's* arrival also replaced the *Caedmon* which was switched to Lymington to operate with her sisters. The *Cuthred* was retained for summer work but when in 1986, a third 'Saint' was ordered, her days were most certainly numbered.

As the Robb yard had closed with the departure of the *St. Helen*, Cochrane of Selby was given the order. The *St. Cecilia* was duly launched on 4th November 1986 and arrived at Portsmouth on 18th March 1987. Not only was she carpeted throughout but there were a number of other modifications carried out in the light of the operation of the first two of the class. The most noticeable difference was in the positioning of the refreshment counter which in the *St. Cecilia* was 'round the corner' from the other two and also much larger, although, as part of an ongoing rolling programme of modification they have recently had this important area modified and resited.

After an inaugural cruise in the Solent on 23rd March, during which time it failed to stop raining, the third 'Saint' entered service on 27th March.

Then with the Lymington Harbour Commissioners preventing further Sealink investment in new ships for the western Solent link, 10th April 1989 saw the order for a £7 million fourth new ferry ready to take the Portsmouth - Fishbourne route into the twenty-first century. The vessel was launched at Selby as the *St. Faith* on 28th March 1990 and entered service on 16th July. A further modification of the class showed itself in an extra outside passenger deck on the same level as the funnel.

ENTER *ST. CLARE*

At the beginning of 2000, Wightlink presented a detailed brief and plan to twenty-three shipyards (four of them British) before ordering a further vehicle ferry for the Fishbourne route. The £11.5 million *St. Clare* was designed by naval architects Hart Fenton and ordered from the Remontowa Yard in Gdansk, Poland - the first Isle of Wight ferry to be built abroad. With capacity for 750 passengers and 180 cars, the new ship offers the dual benefits of faster loading onto two car decks and a mezzanine deck together with the latest on board facilities. The new ship is 86 metres long with a beam of 18 metres (8 metres longer and one metre wider

Looking across the wheelhouse of the **St. Cecilia**, *one of the original 'Saint' class ships. Totally enclosed, it is fitted with all the modern aids and electronics one would find in any sea-going vessel. The bridge wings extend well beyond the ship's sides in order to give the Captain a clear view ahead and astern when manoeuvring. (John Hendy)*

than the earlier 'Saints') and is powered by 4 Wartsila medium speed diesel engines propelling four Voith Schneider units. Her design represents a return to the double-ended type of vessel as seen in the previous generation car ferries built for the Isle of Wight services. With traffic at the Fishbourne and Portsmouth terminals busier than ever before, the double-ended nature of the St. Clare allows for fast turn-round times and minimal delays during busy operational periods - vital ingredients for the continuing success of Wightlink's premier service.

On board, passengers have a choice of two lounges and seating in a range of configurations to cater for different party sizes. The main lounge features a walk-in convenience shop and on the same level there is a food and beverage unit. A second such area exists in the upper lounge alongside a children's area and pets' corner.

New side loading facilities for foot passengers have been provided on the ship but their use awaits development on land.

During the year 2001, Wightlink carried over 1.3 million cars and 50% of all island traffic now crosses on the Portsmouth - Fishbourne service.

The growth on this most important of all the sea-links to the island has been phenomenal and in the years to come it is well-equipped to strengthen its premier position.

The St. Clare arrived at Portsmouth via the Kiel Canal on 16th July and after familiarisation and training trials operated her first commercial sailing to Fishbourne four days later at 14.30.

Operating the Car Ferries
by Captain Dennis Ford

One of the secrets of the car ferry lies in the form of propulsion chosen. Although expensive to install and run, Voith Schneider propellers offer excellent manoeuvrability (including the ability to hold the vessel stationary) under all but the most extreme conditions, without outside help.

The three main engines, situated centrally, drive three propeller units (one forward and two aft) via shafts. Each

*With the tower of Portsmouth Cathedral and the entrance to the Camber Docks astern, the **St. Cecilia** is manoeuvred towards her Gunwharf terminal. (John Hendy)*

propeller unit consists of a set of gears, pumps and valves inside the ship to control a rotor from which five flat (4.5 feet long by 1 foot wide) propeller blades hang vertically down beneath the vessel. The mechanism gives each blade two movements: a continuous rotation with all the other blades as the rotor carrying them turns and its own individual motion twisting back and forth on its own axis (not unlike that of a fishes tail). These two movements when put together are used to produce thrust to pull the vessel in any direction chosen; control being achieved from the wheel-house steering consoles via rods and levers to

A Voith-Schneider propeller ready for fitting. The blades of the IOW units are 4ft 6 in. long. (E.C. Goldsworthy & Co.)

*The **St. Cecilia's** Mezzanine Deck lowered to a gradient of 1 in 7 for cars to disembark at Portsmouth. These half decks (situated either side of the central housing in the four earlier 'Saints') increase carrying capacity by approximately 54 cars. Each one is in two parts and hinged in the middle: drop one end to the Main Deck and drive cars on, raise the level during the crossing and then drop the other end to drive off and disembark. When not required the decks are stowed up out of the way. (John Hendy)*

VOITH SCHNEIDER CAR FERRY PROPULSION

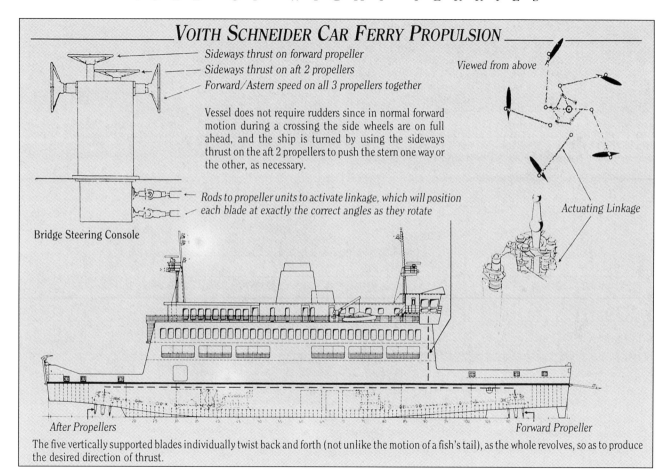

— Sideways thrust on forward propeller
— Sideways thrust on aft 2 propellers
— Forward/Astern speed on all 3 propellers together

Vessel does not require rudders since in normal forward motion during a crossing the side wheels are on full ahead, and the ship is turned by using the sideways thrust on the aft 2 propellers to push the stern one way or the other, as necessary.

Viewed from above

Rods to propeller units to activate linkage, which will position each blade at exactly the correct angles as they rotate

Actuating Linkage

Bridge Steering Console

After Propellers

Forward Propeller

The five vertically supported blades individually twist back and forth (not unlike the motion of a fish's tail), as the whole revolves, so as to produce the desired direction of thrust.

actuate the linkage which will position each blade at exactly the correct angles as they rotate. In practice the benefits of this type of propulsion are both necessary and much used. The relatively short crossing means that a large proportion of the Captain's day is spent in position manoeuvring which, whilst it could often be effected with more conventional methods, allows the ship to be handled at greater speeds and with considerably less risk of damage in a confined space without any help from tugs or ropes.

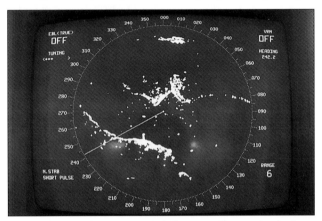

Radar screen taken approximately half way to Fishbourne. The Isle of Wight is at the bottom with Ryde Pier clearly visible. The ship is in the middle of the numbered circle which contains a 'bird's eye' electronic picture of everything within a chosen range. The line from the centre marks the course and the presentation is stabilized to keep north at the top of the screen. Each ship has two radars and can safely navigate in any visibility. (John Hendy)

*The Fishbourne linkspan seen from the wheelhouse of the **St. Cecilia**. Hinged at the shore end, the automatically controlled ramp rises and falls with the tide (tidal range is about 16 feet) by means of four large hydraulic rams. (John Hendy)*

PORTSMOUTH - RYDE
The Fast Link

The local Ryde newspaper for 1st December 1860 recorded the death of Capt. James Groves and relates how, half a century previously, in the company of his late partner, Capt. Beazley, a once a day sailing-boat service was commenced between Portsmouth and Ryde.

The article explains how, about thirty five years previously, Groves and Beazley had introduced the first steam packet, the *Union*, which was followed into service by the *Arrow*.

"All middle-aged inhabitants of Ryde can recollect the great excitement caused by the introduction of steam navigation to our waters" it continued, and asserted that, "Ryde has been metamorphosed from a little fishing village with unpaved, unlighted and unwatched streets into a fashionable and aristocratic town."

As early as 1817 a steamship service had been inaugurated between Portsmouth and Ryde using the 50 ton *Britannia* which was built at Gainsborough in Lincolnshire for the service linking London with Southend. She commenced a twice daily service on 19th May leaving Portsmouth at 08.30 and 17.30 but proved unsuitable for the eastern Solent and was auctioned at Portsmouth on 24th November 1817.

A service offered by the Portsmouth & Ryde Steam Packet Co.

In this print, dated August 1828, a wooden paddle steamer (believed to be the **Arrow***) approaches Ryde Pier with its tow-boat astern. Notice the top-hatted Captain at the stern of the vessel. (John Hendy collection)*

eventually relied upon three small vessels. The first was the Rotherhithe-built *Union* of 1822 which entered service on 5th April 1825. She had previously been working on the Ramsgate - Calais route and on her trials, under the command of Capt. Groves, made the Ryde passage in 34 minutes. She was followed in June by the three year old *Arrow* (a product of the Lang yard at Dumbarton) which unfortunately suffered from heavy coal consumption and was offered for sale in the following year before being disposed of in 1830. The third ship was the *Lord Yarborough* which was the first vessel actually built for the P&RSPCo and entered service in July 1826. She was built at nearby Fishbourne and on a twice-weekly basis would be engaged in excursions linking Cowes and Brighton via Portsmouth and Ryde returning on the following day. A round excursion to Poole was also offered. The ship was eventually sold to a Plymouth coal merchant in 1852. A fourth Portsmouth & Ryde ship was the *Earl Spencer* which was built at Ryde and entered service in June 1833 not being disposed of until 1855.

In order that Ryde Pier could accommodate the new ships, it had been lengthened and enlarged at the cost of £400 in 1824 although in those days the pier was the base for destinations other than Portsmouth.

THE RAILWAY ARRIVES

What changed the developing services even more was the arrival at Gosport of the London & Southampton Railway which opened its new line for traffic on 29th November 1841.

Portsmouth was furious at being served by a railway company which carried the name of a rival port but when it changed its name to the London & South Western Railway, the objections all but ceased.

The Gosport line left the main London - Southampton line at Bishopstoke (now Eastleigh) but due to the uncertainty concerning the stability of the tunnel at Fareham, it was closed four days later and did not reopen until 7th February 1842. An extension from Fareham to Cosham was later built and continued to Portsmouth on 1st October 1848. The coming of the railway saw all Portsmouth - Ryde services based on Gosport in order to meet the trains.

In the summer of 1842 as many as ten sailings a day were

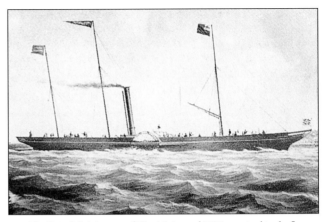

*The United Co's iron vessel **Her Majesty** of 1851 remained in the fleet until 1883 although she was stretched seven years after her launch in order to make her more suitable for excursion work. (Eric Payne collection)*

advertised (4 on Sundays) and the fare structure in those far off days now makes very interesting reading. There were two classes of travel - the exposed Forecastle and the Quarter Deck - for which the public paid 1/- (5p) or 1/6d. (7.5p) Season tickets were available from the captain, a Quarter Deck ticket costing £2-2s-0d.

The Victoria Pier at Old Portsmouth opened for traffic in May 1842 and steadily grew in popularity until the Clarence Pier at Southsea was opened.

Another new structure was the Albert Pier, built in 1846 by the Harbour Pier Company. This stretched some 1,200 ft. out into

Portsmouth Harbour allowing the steamers to land and embark passengers at all states of the tide. Portsmouth Harbour station now occupies this site.

Portsmouth had to wait until 14th June 1847 to receive its first direct railway line when the London Brighton & South Coast Railway pushed through from Havant thereby linking the city with London via Hove. An omnibus would now await the arrival of each train at Portsmouth station and convey passengers to the Victoria Pier for passage to the Isle of Wight.

The new Lymington-built *Prince Albert* joined the fleet in 1847 in anticipation of the increased traffic the new railway would bring, but three years later a rival company, the Portsea, Portsmouth, Gosport and Isle of Wight New Steam Packet Company, introduced its wooden steamers the *Prince of Wales* and the *Princess Royal* from the famous J. Samuel White yard at Cowes. For a while there was much competition, racing, fighting between crews and a large degree of ill-feeling especially after Capt. Groves was held responsible for a collision between his *Prince Albert* and the rival company's *Prince of Wales*.

The original Portsmouth & Ryde Co. now introduced the Millwall-built steamer *Her Majesty*, the first iron vessel to compete with the newcomers but at the end of 1851, sense prevailed and the companies merged. They formed the delightfully named, Port of Portsmouth & Ryde United Steam Packet Company which was usually abbreviated to the 'United Co.'

The new ships saw off two of the original vessels but the *Union* was retained, one presumes as a relief ship. In July 1851, 5 hour trips round the island were offered every Monday and Thursday

The **Prince of Wales** at anchor off Ryde Pier possibly on tow-boat duty. *(Eric Payne collection)*

costing 3/6d. or 2/6d. if travelling on the open Foredeck.

The early years of the United Co. appear to have been a wretched time for communications to the island.

In March 1855 the "Isle of Wight Observer's" great disgust was levelled at the company after a fare of 5/- (25p) was charged for an excursion to accompany the Baltic Fleet out to the Nab. Amends were made a week later however when 6d. and 8d. was charged for a Sunday excursion around the fleet in Spithead which, "found favour in the eyes of all classes."

Then in May 1856 a letter appeared from one of 40 passengers who had gone on an excursion to Netley on Southampton Water to witness the occasion of the laying of the foundation stone at the Royal Victoria Hospital. Not only did the steamer arrive too late to be of any use but she berthed at Hamble instead!

At the end of 1856, the United Co. announced the enlargement of *Her Majesty* and the *Princess Royal* after successful alterations carried out to the *Prince of Wales*, but even this failed to impress the public.

In May 1857, another letter in the "Isle of Wight Observer" complained that nearly seven years previously the writer had crossed from Portsmouth to Ryde in 20 minutes at a fare of 8d. in the *Prince of Wales*. He had recently crossed again in the same ship and in similar weather but for 10d. and in 42 minutes. "What can be the reason for this retrograde movement?" he demanded.

December 1857 saw another attack. "Out of five boats, there is not one fit to send on the passage. Who is responsible for such neglect?" These comments were made after the writer had crossed in "that old tub, the *Union*" which took 55 minutes from Ryde to Portsea. The writer observed that the base of her furnace was burnt out so they could keep no fire with which to make steam. The return crossing to Ryde that evening took 80 minutes, and on a cold winter's night, the completely open decks of the spartan steamers could have given very little in the way of protection from the weather. The route's first regular steam-powered vessel was later sold and converted into a sailing ship before being broken up in 1863.

Things had not improved by May 1858 when it was stated that of the five vessels in the United Co.'s fleet, not one was fit to work

the passage. On Whit Monday, the Southampton Co.'s *Medina* was actually chartered to work the United Co.'s excursion around the Isle of Wight.

The local press gave details early in 1858 concerning the stretching of the steamer *Her Majesty*- "the United Co.'s favourite boat." She was heightened between her decks which were carried out over the paddle sponsons to give greater accommodation for excursions. It was also noted in the partisan "Observer" that a Mr. Pratt of Ryde gave excellent on-board catering.

August 1858 saw excursions operated to Cherbourg but the "Observer" claimed that the directors of the United Co. "have a policy of saving at the spigot and letting out at the bunghole" - squandering money at Portsmouth but too mean to advertise their timetable in the Isle of Wight.

This theme was continued the following June after the *Her Majesty's* first trip of the season around the island which the directors failed to advertise in the Wight. Consequently few were aware of the sailing and passengers were thin. However, "Mr. Pratt's abundant collation gave every satisfaction".

September 1859 saw a series of excursions to see Brunel's new *Great Eastern* at Portland for 6/- (30p) return. Unfortunately the trips were not advertised in Ryde and so the thousands of visitors knew nothing about it. On one occasion the ship took just 10 passengers.

The United Co.'s first new ship for the Portsmouth - Ryde link was the *Prince Consort*. Although due in service on 10th August 1859 she was not launched at Millwall until early October, quite complete and with steam up. She arrived on station at the end of

*The United Co's last ship was the pretty **Alexandra**. Built in 1879, she was "finished more like a yacht than a passenger steamer." Sold in 1913, she is seen here in the ownership of Cosens of Weymouth to whom she passed in September 1914. (George Cook collection)*

the month and over the Stokes Bay measured mile attained a full speed of 18.5 knots.

Measuring 145 ft. by 14 ft. and with 60 h.p. engines, the *Prince Consort's* contract price was £5,000.

LONDON-PORTSMOUTH DIRECT

The new ship was built to coincide with the opening of the London & South Western Railway's direct London - Portsmouth railway line via Guildford and Petersfield. The final section from Godalming to Havant opened on 1st January 1859 but the section from Havant to Portsmouth was owned by the rival London Brighton & South Coast Railway and action in the law courts was necessary before running powers over the Brighton line were obtained ready for the first through train on 24th January. It was a great improvement saving 20 miles on the earlier route.

At the end of the year, the *Her Majesty* was off service with paddle-float damage and so the *Prince of Wales* was reactivated even though she had previously been condemned by the Board of Trade as being unsafe! In spite of this handicap, she was sent off to visit the *Great Eastern* and is claimed to have made excellent time.

In the spring of 1861, the "Observer" gave an account of the United Co.'s fleet. The *Prince Consort*, the crack craft of the company, had been alongside Gosport Pier all winter and "suffered to go as she pleases" being covered in rust and dirt. The *Prince Albert* was, "the worst boat the company ever owned" and had so little paint that the paper claimed that she would look better with none at all! The *Prince of Wales* was "viley shabby" and in service, while the *Princess Royal* was sharing the drudgery of the towing work and was unpainted, unwashed and minus her figurehead which had been lost in a collision. It was stated that she would be disgraceful in appearance alongside a river tug. Concerning *Her Majesty*, "her deck is in a beastly condition, her hull is unscrubbed and unfit for service, in sharp contrast to the Southampton boats which are always kept in summer order." The article went on to say that competition would be welcomed with open arms on the Ryde route and what was wanted were clean and decent boats.

A railway line linking Gosport with Stokes Bay was opened in April 1863, the former town having lost its pier in the previous February when the Government purchased it and converted it to a coastguard station. The United Co. later chartered a ship to the railway company in order that a service to Ryde might be offered. The link continued until 1913.

The *Her Majesty*, "one of the best and fastest boats of the company" had the misfortune to hit the Coal Rocks between Bembridge and the Nab whilst engaged on a round the island excursion in August 1863. The vessel was beached at Lane End and the passengers were ferried ashore by pilot boat. The steamer was eventually taken to the Camber at Portsmouth and repaired at a

*Seen alongside at Ryde, the **Victoria** was the first of the Joint Railway Co's fleet. Entering service in 1881, she was a double-ender in order to save time by turning in harbour. (George Cook collection)*

cost of £1,000.

She was again in the news in January 1865 when a mechanical fault put her out of service and the company was forced to bring in the dilapidated *Princess Royal*, "so rickety as to be hardly able to move even in smooth water."

But in April, the United Co. were asking for designs for a new iron paddle steamer and offered a prize of £25 for the winner!

The new ship was the £5,000 *Princess of Wales* which was delivered on 28th August 1865. She was, said the press, fitted in a manner far superior to any other vessel on the passage and crossed between Southsea and Ryde in just 19 minutes.

However, by the end of October the directors announced that they were not satisfied either with her speed or in the way in

*The **Duchess of Edinburgh** was one of a pair of double-ended ships with funnels side by side. She is seen here late in her career in August 1910 carrying the funeral cortege of the Bishop of Portsmouth. Notice the flags at half mast. (Eric Payne collection)*

which she was fitted out.

The vessel was sent to Southampton to be looked at and a series of alterations were set in hand. Her two boilers, which had increased her running costs to £12-14s-0d. above the rest of the fleet were reduced to one and her deck capacity thereby increased by 25ft. on the foredeck. It was claimed that the vessel was not watertight, at least 6ft. too narrow and certainly not up to contract! One wonders just how the winner of the competition to design her decided to spend his prize money! The builders were Lewis & Stockwell of London.

However, the year 1865 marked a watershed in the history of the United Co. If their performance up until now had been less than satisfactory it was noted in the local press that breakdowns were now almost unheard of whilst two years previously they had been a daily occurrence. The service now offered was remarkably intense - the summer of 1865 seeing no less than 46 daily arrivals and departures at Ryde Pier, although not all of them were by the United Company.

An interesting development began in June 1866 when arrangements were completed for the conveyance of passengers and parcels from Ryde to Fishbourne in rowing and sailing boats.

Early 1868 saw the thirty month old *Princess of Wales* having a

*Entering service in 1890 came the **Duchess of Albany**, seen approaching Ryde Pier. (Eric Payne collection)*

*The **Southsea** of 1948 was the Portsmouth - Ryde link's first motor vessel and served the passage for a faithful forty years. (John Hendy)*

The new flagship **St. Clare** *passing through the narrows at the entrance to Portsmouth Harbour in September 2001. (John Hendy)*

*Built at Southampton in 1897, the **Duchess of Kent** was the first of the more enclosed and larger steamers carrying as many as 870 passengers. (Eric Payne collection)*

at Blackwall and, as the *Duke of Edinburgh,* she arrived at Portsmouth in April 1869. A special trials trip was completed on 22nd April when the vessel paddled to Alum Bay.

It was claimed that she was built for speed and crossed from Portsmouth to Ryde in just 18 minutes. Her accommodation was "superior" with a superbly fitted saloon, mirrors and crimson velvet seats. However, it was noted that she did appear to roll rather much and was a wet ship. Under ballasting was said to be the problem.

On her first day in service, the *Duke of Edinburgh* crossed from Ryde in a little under 17 minutes. She measured 136 ft. by 14 ft. 2 in. by 7 ft. and cost £3,950.

Sistership *Princess Alice* came on station at the end of June at which time the "Duke" went away to receive modifications to reduce rolling.

During the early part of 1870, the United Co. sent the *Princess of Wales* into the Camber Docks for extensive alterations and improvements. This type of ship surgery is fairly common today but was a most unusual occurrence then. The ship was cut in two and received an extra 12 ft. in order to stretch her. New boilers

new £550 boiler fitted. It will be remembered that the one removed was originally one of a pair which, in order to reach the required power, had been worked hard.

The end of the year saw the old *Prince Albert* put up for sale. There being no buyer, the ship was dismantled and the engines put in store. A further new ship was now ordered from Messrs. Wigram made her the fastest ship on the route and with her extra accommodation, 500 passengers could now be carried. She was launched from Mr. Read's slipway in early April, after the work (which cost £1,000) was completed.

In late May, the *Prince of Wales* was in collision off Portsmouth with the collier *Sunderland*. She was fortunately without any passengers on board at the time and had it not been for a nearby sandbank, on which she was grounded, the paddler would have sunk.

The *Duke of Edinburgh* and the *Prince Consort* were required by the Admiralty to attempt to tow off the training ship H.M.S. *Racer* from Ryde bank after she had stranded during mid-September 1871. In this task they failed and proved that they were more successful as ferries than tugs.

The *Prince Consort* was again in the news on the last day of 1871 when just off Southsea she struck a submerged sewer, holing her bottom and inspite of valiant attempts to keep her afloat, she sank two days later. Although she was not raised for a further week, she was eventually taken to the Camber and repaired. It was obviously a bad week for the United Co. as the *Her Majesty* and *Prince of Wales* collided with each other off Ryde.

During the autumn of 1872, a new company - the Southsea and Isle of Wight Steam Ferry Company Ltd. - was founded to operate a half-hourly service between Southsea and Ryde. John White of East Cowes was contracted to build the company's first three steamers, the *Ventnor, Shanklin* and *Ryde* while Stephen Lampard of Portsea constructed the *Southsea* - this being the first instance of vessels being given the names of local towns.

The *Princess Louise* joined the United Co. fleet in August 1873 having been built on the Thames by Messrs. Lewis & Stockwell. She was claimed to be a "fine screw boat" but rolled too much to be appreciated. Her sistership, the *Princess Beatrice* appeared in the following May.

Meanwhile the opposition Southsea & Ryde Steam Ferry Co. launched their *Shanklin* and *Ventnor* on 15th May 1873 while the *Ryde* followed on 27th June. It was claimed that their economy of fuel, ease of management and the great passenger accommodation would ensure their success.

The first two of the series commenced operations on 5th July and from the start charged fares which greatly undercut the United Co.

September 1874 saw a letter to the editor of the "Isle of Wight Times" signed by no less than one hundred people complaining that they had been let down by the captain of the *Princess of Wales* who only took them as far as the Needles when their excursion was advertised as round the Isle of Wight. The Master had claimed that the swells of the previous day's gales would have made for an uncomfortable passage with heavy rolling.

However, the captain was to get his own back as two days later about 50 people embarked for an excursion to Bournemouth in very rough seas and in a near gale. Determined this time not to upset his passengers, the captain succeeded in drenching almost everyone on board. So bad was the weather that the engine room skylight was washed off and thrown into the saloon.

At the close of 1874, the United Co. made a decision to withdraw their two recent screw steamers which had proved unsuitable for the traffic and were disliked and avoided by the public.

During April 1875, the United Co. purchased for £8,500, the second hand and three year old paddle steamer *Heather Bell* which was claimed to be splendidly fitted-out with "most luxurious cabins". The local press said of her, "she is the most complete ship in every respect, and beyond doubt surpasses any boat seen in these waters." At 200 ft. in length, she was the largest vessel to run the Portsmouth - Ryde passage until then. She was widely used on excursions (and even ran to Cherbourg) but her fleet companion, the *Princess Alice* received some very bad press that June when, on leaving Ryde Pier, the ladies and gentlemen sitting abaft of the funnel were unexpectedly showered with a mixture of salt water and grease - the result of filling the boiler too full with sea water!

But the year 1875 saw passengers on the Portsmouth - Ryde link better catered for than ever before with the new *Heather Bell* releasing the previous excursion ships (*Princess of Wales* and *Prince Consort*) for the ferry traffic. The rest of the fleet received refits, new engines and new boilers.

Competition between the United Co. and the Southsea & Isle of Wight Ferry Co. was proving to be pointless and negotiations were going on in October 1875 to put an end to it.

In the autumn of 1877 the Southsea Co. was wound up after having made heavy losses. Their last steamer (the *Southsea*) had cost as much as £6,700 while for several months the average receipts were £3-6s-0d and expenses over £30. The company and its ships were purchased by the United Co.

In an effort to assure its customers of the continuing good service, the United Co. now ordered a new steamer from the Southampton yard of Messrs. Oswald Mordaunt & Co. The *Albert Edward* was launched with due ceremony on 25th May 1878. She was 170 ft. long with a beam of 20 ft. and gave covered seating for both first and second class passengers. Her 17 ft. diameter paddle wheels were driven at 45 revolutions a minute and she earned the reputation as being a very fast steamer.

THE JOINT COMPANY

The beginning of the end for the old United Co. occurred in March 1879 when the London & South Western and Brighton & South Coast railways applied to Parliament for a Bill allowing them to run steamboats from Portsmouth to the Isle of Wight. In October 1876, they had opened the line between Portsmouth Town and Portsmouth Harbour stations and in an attempt to extend their influence, sought to run the steamer services to the island making it known that the United Co. was not welcome, unless in case of emergency, at the new Portsmouth Harbour railway pier.

Rather than sit back to await its fate, the United Co. went onto the attack by ordering a new ship from the well-known Scottish yard of Scott & Co. of Greenock while the *Heather Bell* was also sent back to the Clyde for new boilers and machinery.

The new ship was the *Alexandra* which entered service in mid-June 1879. It was noted that she was finished more like a yacht than a passenger steamer and at the end of the year, the company's second half-yearly meeting heard that she had proved to be a valuable and successful addition to the fleet. It was noted at the same time that the four screw ships taken over from the erstwhile Southsea & Isle of Wight Ferry Co. had all been sold, "at some sacrifice".

Since the opening of Portsmouth Harbour station, the United Co.'s losses had been substantial and an unsuccessful attempt had been made to enter into a trading union with the Southampton Co. (operators of the Southampton - Cowes link).

The days of the United Co. were now numbered with the South Western and Brighton & South Coast Railway companies giving orders for four large steam packets able to cut the crossing times down from 25 to 18 minutes. They had, in 1879, obtained an Act of Parliament empowering them to purchase the steamers and work the passage at an estimated cost of £100,000. The two main line railway companies also planned to purchase the whole of the Isle of Wight railway system in addition to the new railway pier at Ryde then under construction.

In the February of 1880, both the running powers on the Ryde - Portsmouth link plus the United Co. fleet of seven vessels were sold to the mainland railway companies for £38,000. The actual takeover occurred during early April although nothing changed apart from the name of the new operating company which was, in future, to be referred to as, "The Joint Railway Companies' Steampacket Service."

The first great bonus for the new Joint Company was the opening of the new railway pier at Ryde on 12th July 1880. For the first time, trains could now bring their passengers right to the boats which not only made the greatest of differences to passengers but also to luggage and cargo handling although heavy cargo and

*The **Duchess of Fife** (1899) soon gained a tremendous reputation for her sea-going qualities. (Eric Payne collection)*

livestock continued to use the timeless horseboats.

However, it was not long before the residents of Ryde expressed their dissatisfaction with their improved service, complaining at a public meeting during November that trains did not always wait for late boats and that boats did not always wait for late trains. Needless to say, this complaint survives until the present day!

The first vessel built for the Joint Companies fleet was the *Victoria* which arrived from the Clyde on 2nd November 1881 and which presented an odd sight being the first true double-ended

*The **Duchess of Norfolk** joined the service in 1911. Her sister became a war loss hitting a mine during sweeping operations in 1919. (Eric Payne collection)*

vessel on the Solent in order to avoid the necessity of turning in harbours and confined spaces. Costing some £17,300 to build, the *Victoria* created a tremendous impression, providing a degree of luxury which regular travellers to the Isle of Wight were unused to. Her length of 191 ft. and beam across the paddle boxes of 45.5 ft. made for a high degree of stability for the 700 or so passengers that she carried although she gained a reputation for being "a wet boat" in any sea and her saloons were soon reserved for the First Class passengers only.

Two more double-enders followed in 1884, built in the same Aitken & Mansell yard at Whiteinch. The first was the *Duchess of Edinburgh* (launched on 9th April) and the second, the *Duchess of Connaught*, was launched on 29th April. Both were designed by the celebrated Victorian railway engineer Mr. William Stroudley of the London Brighton & South Coast Railway, the man who had introduced feathering paddle floats which enabled the steamers to gain maximum speed from their engines, as they entered the water at right-angles and exercised full thrust.

The first of the new steamers completed her successful trials trip in the Solent on 27th June 1884. She was in every way, an improved *Victoria* giving the Second Class passengers far more shelter than before and costing in the region of £20,000. Sistership *Duchess of Connaught* arrived on station at the end of July.

Entering service with the Joint Co. in 1890 came the *Duchess of Albany*. She was built at Scott of Greenock and during trials on the Clyde in early January managed a speed of 14 knots. She was claimed to be an improved *Alexandra* and measured 170 ft. by 22 ft. with a certificate for 400 passengers. The practice of building double-enders was ceased as the idea had not proved a success.

Sistership *Princess Margaret* followed in 1893 and early in her service managed the passage between Stokes Bay and Ryde in just 11 minutes and from Ryde to Southsea in 16.5 minutes.

The much larger *Duchess of Kent* joined the fleet in 1897 and was a product of Day Summers & Co. of Southampton. Capable of carrying as many as 870 passengers, she was fitted with all the latest improvements and entered service early in September. She was used to supplement the excursion sailings but a spanking new excursion steamer came on station in 1899 in the form of the *Duchess of Fife*.

*The Southern Railway's first contribution to the service was the **Shanklin** which joined the link in 1924.*

This vessel was built by the Clydebank Engineering & Shipbuilding Co. and was ample evidence of the increasing patronage which not only Southsea but all the island resorts were receiving.

She soon gained a tremendous reputation for being the finest of sea boats and would attempt her round the island sailings in weather which kept her rivals within the sheltered waters of the Solent. Her master, the colourful Capt. Charles Gubbey looked as impressive as the ship he commanded and it was said of him that if his full beard was tucked inside his greatcoat then passengers were due for a rough passage. If his beard was outside then the seas would be calm!

On 15th August 1903 the *Duchess of Albany* was in collision with the steam yacht *Wintonia* at the entrance to Portsmouth Harbour. The 'Duchess' was found to be at fault but the findings of the court of inquiry made the point that the Captain and the officer of the watch should have an exclusive position on the ship to themselves and not be mixed up with the passengers. From now on, proper forward view bridges were constructed with unobstructed views of the sea.

In January 1905 a complaint appeared in the "Isle of Wight Mercury" concerning the comfort of people using the boats during the hours of dark. Some of the older steamers were very inadequately lit with an oil lamp placed amidships on either side of the engine room the only illumination available. The writer commented that for the studiously inclined, the passages made life very difficult.

The strong tidal flows through the entrance to Portsmouth Harbour have caused many incidents over the years and on 3rd September 1909 the *Duchess of Kent* was in collision with collier *Transporter*. The "Kent" immediately began taking in water and the Master had no alternative but to beach her on the shingle close to the Victoria Pier. All 400 passengers were safely taken off in boats before the ship filled and sank.

Two days later the ship was salved, patched-up and sailed under her own steam to Southampton, the engine room fortunately not being flooded.

Another collision early in the following March involved the *Princess Margaret*. Swinging in the harbour, she was caught by the tide and carried on to the moored destroyer *Crane* holing her port bow and carrying away her davits and a lifeboat. She continued to Ryde and then sailed to Newhaven for repairs.

D. & W. Henderson of Port Glasgow supplied a pair of fine steamers for the route in 1910- 11 in the form of the *Duchess of Richmond* and *Duchess of Norfolk* With a length of 198 ft. and a beam of 26 ft., the first of the twins was launched during late June 1910 and in anticipation of the second ship, the double-ended twins of 1884 were withdrawn.

*The **Portsdown** and **Merstone** (pictured) entered service in 1928. Both remained on station during the war, the **Portsdown** hitting a mine and being lost off Southsea in September 1941. (Eric Payne collection)*

The local paper recorded the demise of the *Duchess of Connaught* and the *Duchess of Edinburgh* as "those favourite double-enders', which had gone away to Holland never to return. "Many people" the paper continued, "will heave a sigh of relief at the departure (long deferred) of these relics of Ryde's gay youth" on the evening of 17th October.

During the winter of 1913 - 14 something at last was done to improve the lighting in the *Duchess of Albany* and *Princess Margaret*. It was pointed out by the Joint Railway Co. that they could not afford and were not prepared to run the bigger boats during the winter months hence the long-overdue improvements

*The **Southsea** and **Whippingham** were built mainly as excursion steamers in 1930. The first ship (illustrated on builders' trials) was lost off the Tyne while minesweeping in February 1941. (John Hendy collection)*

SOUTHERN RAILWAY

On New Years Day 1923, the Southern Railway Co. came into being and took over the operation of the steamers. Things were slow to change although a buff funnel with black top replaced the white, black-topped funnels of the Joint Railway Co's. fleet.

A replacement for the lost *Duchess of Richmond* was ordered from J.I. Thornycroft's yard at Southampton and launched on 6th June 1924. The vessel was named *Shanklin* and although she was very much built on the lines of the previous steamers for the Ryde route, her name was that of an island railway centre, a theme which became so loved in the years to come.

As with all these early steamers, the First Class was arranged aft while Second Class passengers were accommodated in the forward section. The First Class smoke room was upholstered in green buffalo hide with gold damask curtains at the door and side lights. Even the lavatory fittings were of St. Anne's marble and

to the oldest ships in the fleet. A new smoking room was fitted aft, lavatory accommodation was modernised, a ladies cabin was provided in addition to more shelter for passengers in bad weather. In answer to the complaints of eight years previous, both vessels were fitted throughout with electric lighting.

During the Great War the refurbished sisters maintained the Portsmouth - Ryde passage while the more modern units were called-up, mostly serving as minesweepers. It was in this role that the *Duchess of Richmond* was lost while in the Mediterranean on 28th June 1919 having only served for four years on the Ryde passage.

*Seen on trials on the Firth of Clyde, the **Ryde** was the route's final paddle steamer.*

*Portsmouth Harbour shortly before the war with the **Sandown** arriving from the island.*

thought had been given to reduce heat and noise from the engine room by fully insulating the machinery bulkheads. Measuring 190ft. by 26ft. the 399 gross tons paddle steamer was given a Class III passenger certificate to allow circumnavigation of the island as in those days these excursions were increasingly popular.

The similar steamers *Merstone* and *Portsdown* were ordered in the autumn of 1927 from the Caledon yard at Dundee and replaced the *Duchess of Albany* and *Princess Margaret* on the passage. The *Merstone* was launched on 26th January 1928 making her maiden voyage on 8th May. With capacity for 723, as against the 'Albany's' 479 the increase again pointed to a buoyant tourist trade.

New features in the vessel included a bridge-house for the Captain and far more shelter for Second Class passengers.

The temperature in the saloons could be regulated by use of thermotanks and the First Class saloon was finished in polished oak with seats upholstered in bronze velvet. Sistership *Portsdown* was launched at Dundee on 23rd March and entered service during

June.

The twins represented only a small part of the Southern Railway's £2 million improvement plan for the Isle of Wight.

The much-loved excursion steamer *Duchess of Fife* was disposed of in 1929 and in her place, the Southern introduced two excellent vessels in the form of the *Southsea* and *Whippingham*. They were built at Fairfield's Govan yard on the Clyde and were launched on 2nd April and 1st May respectively.

The *Southsea* was first on station making her inaugural trip on the afternoon of 15th May 1930. Following final adjustments at Southampton, she crossed directly to Ryde in 59 minutes. After being open for inspection, she proceeded to Clarence Pier, Southsea and thence to Portsmouth Harbour where she was welcomed by the ringing of the ships' bells on board the *Portsdown* and *Merstone* which were nearby. At 254 ft. in length and 58 ft. in the beam over the paddles, the new steamer dwarfed her fleet companions and could carry as many as 1,182 passengers at 16 knots.

She was superbly fitted-out with oak, ebony and mahogany being used and far more shelter than previously made certain that her passengers would enjoy their cruises even in poor weather. The Promenade Deck extended the whole length of the vessel and even allowed luggage to be sheltered when the ship was engaged on the ferry route. The 'Isle of Wight County Press' stated that the *Southsea* was "a praiseworthy example of modern genius in design and craftsmanship". She operated her first excursion on 19th May calling at Southsea and Ryde on a trip to Southampton to view the White Star Liner *Olympic* (the *Titanic's* sister).

Down the ways at Denny's Dumbarton yard in March 1948 goes the **Brading.** *Sister* **Southsea** *can be seen in the distance having been launched minutes earlier. The twins were the route's first diesel vessels and the first to be launched for British Railways. (John Hendy collection)*

Following the *Whippingham's* arrival on station only two of the Joint Service Co.'s 'Duchesses' were left in service - the 'Kent' and the 'Norfolk'.

The fates are no kinder to the latest ship in service than they were to the older ones. Evidence of this was the grounding of the *Whippingham* off Sandown Pier on 14th September 1931 when returning from a cruise around the island at low water. Although many of the passengers were landed in an effort to lighten the steamer, she eventually floated off ninety minutes later on a rising tide.

Sister *Southsea*, again on a round the island excursion, with 455 passengers on board was disabled off Brook and driven towards the shore on 7th September 1932. Another excursion ship, the *Emperor of India* found her flying distress signals and quite helpless following the snapping of the main arm of her port paddle wheel. She was fortunately taken in tow and was later transferred to a tug off St. Catherine's Point before finally arriving at Southsea.

The old *Duchess of Kent* was sold in 1933 to the New Medway Steam Packet Co. and traded as the *Clacton Queen*. Then 36 years young, she must have been thought to be in in outstanding condition but only worked for her new owners for two seasons before being resold. She was broken up in 1937.

Taking the 'Kent's' place in the fleet came the *Sandown*, a product of Denny's Dumbarton yard. She was the sixth new vessel for the route in ten years and whereas in 1933 over 2.2 million passengers had used the Portsmouth - Ryde route, only 843,000 had been carried twenty years earlier.

The *Sandown* was launched on 1st May 1934 and on 25th June

*Not a pretty sight. In February 1965, the **Brading** is seen as she briefly appeared in the new British Rail livery. (Tom Rayner)*

received an official welcome at Sandown Pier after which she sailed on her maiden trip from Sandown and Shanklin out into the Channel for ninety minutes at a cost of 1/6d. (7.5p). With an overall length of 223 ft. and a beam of 29 ft. the new steamer's gross tonnage was 684.

During the inter-war years, the Southern frequently arranged liner visits at Southampton and with the growing interest in trans-Atlantic travel, many excursions were operated to meet the increasingly large giants of the seas somewhere off the Nab and to follow them into Southampton. On the evening of 28th April 1935, the *Southsea* and the *Sandown* went to meet the new French liner *Normandie* on her maiden voyage. She anchored in Ryde Roads at about 23.20 but in spite of the hour, both ships were crowded and were joined by a host of other pleasure craft. The late Eric Payne wrote, "This was a truly magnificent sight, the ship a blaze of light from every window and porthole and her three huge funnels, and the vapour from them being floodlit together with the superstructure. There seemed to be craft everywhere, whistles and sirens frequently sending out their greetings. It was a sight never to be forgotten!"

But the 1935 summer season was once more to be marred by the breakdown of one of the new excursion ships. On 5th September, some six miles off the Needles, the *Whippingham* bound for Bournemouth with some 400 passengers on board damaged a paddle wheel in rising seas. A destroyer and two other excursion steamers went to her aid before the Lymington steamer *Freshwater* came upon the scene and attempted to tow her large fleet companion. Then the last of the 'Duchesses', the *Duchess of Norfolk* arrived at haste from Portsmouth and in spite of the tow rope parting twice, she managed to pull the stricken vessel into the smoother waters off Yarmouth where the *Southsea* was on hand and the passengers were transferred.

The problems weren't over as on 27th August the following year, the *Southsea* with 700 passengers damaged her starboard paddle almost a mile off the Forelands at Bembridge and was unable to proceed. The *Sandown* was sent to assist and towed the larger steamer towards Portsmouth. It was claimed that the paddle had hit a submerged underwater object causing the fracturing of one of the main arms of the wheel.

Floating wreckage also caused damage to the *Portsdown* after she had left Ryde Pier for Portsmouth on the last Saturday in

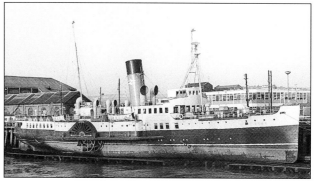

*The **Ryde** undergoing overhaul at Newhaven in March 1969. (John Hendy)*

February 1937. Her sister, the *Merstone*, attempted to tow the striken vessel but it was too rough although eventually a tug did manage to do so but the *Portsdown* did not arrive at Portsmouth until 17.00 - rather too late for the football match to which many of the passengers were travelling!

A sister to the *Sandown* was ordered from Denny of Dumbarton. The *Ryde* was launched on 23rd April 1937 and completed her official maiden voyage on 1st July although she appears to have been in service for at least a fortnight previously. Her entry into service coincided with the arrival of the first electric train at Portsmouth Harbour thus speeding up connections from the capital and the island.

The *Ryde* was given rather more deck space than her sister and had a certificate for 1,050 passengers. She was 223 ft. long with a beam of 29 ft. and was the very last of the traditional paddle steamers which had served the island so faithfully for so many years. With the *Ryde* in service, the *Duchess of Norfolk* was sold to Messrs. Cosens of Weymouth and as their *Embassy* she continued until 1967 - a wonderful career of 56 years.

The outbreak of war in 1939 saw the more modern units requisitioned for use as minesweepers, their shallow draft making them ideal for this purpose.

H.M.S. *Sandown's* record certainly makes exciting reading and if her crew ever thought that the humdrum ferry routine between Ryde and Portsmouth verged on the boring, there must have been many times within the following few years when they wished again for the quiet life of Spithead.

The *Sandown* was leader of the 10th Minesweeping Flotilla operating out of Dover. She evacuated British troops from Holland and during the evacuation of Dunkirk in May and June 1940, saved 3,000 men.

During her minesweeping career she was attacked by no fewer than twenty-two dive bombers at different times and over one hundred bombs were dropped in her direction. Her closest scrape came when a mine blew up close to her stern, the force of which threw up her stern and buried her bows into the sea. The see-saw motion then sent her stern under and the engine room was flooded to a depth of 2 ft. The ship was later converted to a heavily armed ack-ack vessel and was present during the Normandy landings of June 1944.

Others were not so fortunate. The three older vessels, *Shanklin*, *Portsdown* and *Merstone* were left to continue the ferry service and in the early morning of 20th September 1941 the *Portsdown* hit a mine and was lost off Southsea after which time the ancient *Solent* (of 1902) was brought up from Lymington to assist on the Ryde passage. The other casualty was the splendid *Southsea* which was run ashore near the River Tyne on 16th February 1941 after hitting a mine. She was later declared a total loss.

The *Ryde* was the first ship back on station after the war on the 7th July 1945 and was followed shortly afterwards by the *Sandown*. The *Whippingham* followed in 1946 but no more would she be used for the long sea cruises as in pre-war years. Instead, her wings were clipped and cruises were confined to within the Solent. She became increasingly heavy on coal and although very useful on peak summer Saturdays, she saw less work as the fifties progressed.

NATIONALISATION

Ordered by the Southern Railway but launched after the Nationalisation of the railways (on New Years Day 1948) there now came a pair of quite revolutionary vessels for the Portsmouth - Ryde link.

The twin screw motor vessels *Southsea* and *Brading* were

launched at Denny's Dumbarton yard within half an hour of each other on 11th March 1948 and the first of the new twins arrived at Southampton for local trials during mid-October. With a length of 200 ft. and a beam of 47 ft. the new ships were exceptionally broad in relationship to their length - a ratio of 1:4.5. Passenger certificates for 1,331 in two classes were to make them the largest ships ever built for the route and each cost in the region of £160,000.

A press trip on 19th October was followed by entry into service of the *Southsea* on the first day of November and it did not take long before the value of her new radar was to prove itself. During one of the worst fogs for years, when the island would normally have been totally cut off from the mainland - the *Southsea* was the only ferry to attempt passage to the island and soon became a very popular vessel.

The *Brading* entered service on 2nd December 1948 and proved her worth at the end of the following October. On this occasion, the *Ryde* was the last boat to leave Ryde Pier at 21.30. An hour later, Portsmouth telephoned to ask where she was! Later still the *Ryde* berthed back at the pier, the Master announcing that he had been stuck in fog off the entrance to Portsmouth Harbour. The *Brading* was sent out to assist and on berthing at Ryde, embarked the luckless passengers. Shortly after 23.00 she left for the mainland with the *Ryde* directly astern being guided by "the magic eye of radar'. By the time that the ships arrived off Portsmouth, the fog had disappeared!

On 1st December 1950 the venerable *Shanklin* completed her final Ryde - Portsmouth run and was sent to lay-up at Southampton where she was offered for sale. Cosens of Weymouth were obviously so well pleased with their previous purchases (the *Alexandra* and *Duchess of Norfolk/Embassy*) that they bought the *Shanklin* and renamed her *Monarch*. In this role she lasted until the end of the 1960 season.

A third motor vessel was by this time building at Dumbarton and took the name *Shanklin*. She was launched on 22nd February 1951 and entered service on 18th June. She was a one class ship and from that day, her fleet companions also became one class only.

The *Merstone* was withdrawn from service in September 1952

The motor vessel **Shanklin** *joined the link in June 1951 and introduced one class travel. She is seen approaching the mainland in September 1965. (John Hendy collection)*

leaving the service in the hands of the three new diesels and the three 1930's paddle steamers.

The *Whippingham* was finally retired at the end of the 1962 season while at the end of 1964, British Railways became British Rail and introduced a new livery for their fleet. The time-honoured black hulls became blue, the white upperworks were repainted a grey while the historic buff, black topped funnels were repainted red on which the double arrow logo of the revamped B.R. appeared below the black top. The *Brading* was the first Isle of Wight vessel in the new livery and was briefly used as a test-bed for a quite dreadful application of it. Fortunately sense prevailed, the blue section of the bull was lowered and the pale grey upperworks colour, with which three local vessels were daubed, was repainted white.

The *Sandown* lasted one year in the new colours before being towed away for scrapping in Belgium leaving the *Ryde* alone as the last paddle steamer in the Solent.

The three diesel ferries all received long-overdue facelifts during the spring of 1967. A Spar Deck was fitted with seats for 170 passengers as a continuation of the Bridge Deck. Internally there were other changes involving the two lounges on the Main Deck. The bar/cafeteria was moved from the after lounge into the forward one and in order to give extra space for the modified catering arrangements, plus 100 seats, a section of the hold was reclaimed and extra wide windows were fitted in line with the existing ones. Seating throughout the three ships was renewed and refurbished.

One hundred and fifty two years of history ended on 13th September 1969 when the paddle steamer *Ryde* was withdrawn from service. She was eventually sold for static use on the River Medina, between East Cowes and Newport where she remains forgotten and forlorn.

A second major refit was carried out on the three diesels during their overhauls at Immingham in the winter of 1973/4. Steelwork was gritblasted and passenger accommodation throughout was modified with the addition of formica tables and vinyl-covered walls. At the same time, the amidships sections of the Promenade Decks were also plated over to allow the new mechanical gangways both at Portsmouth and Ryde to rest on them. The introduction of the wide ramps had sped up loading enormously and it was now possible to turn a ferry around in just fifteen minutes. The modifications cost some £100,000 for each ship.

Although a large sum of money was later spent on the *Shanklin* to make her more suitable for cruising, annoying engine problems now beset her and she was officially withdrawn from service on 6th March 1980.

With only two passenger ships now available for the Ryde service, the summer season saw all cruises and calls at Clarence Pier, Southsea, dropped from the timetable.

Now 32 years old, it was apparent that the *Southsea* and *Brading* could not soldier on for too many years and British Rail looked at ways in which they could replace them.

FAST CRAFT

British Rail Hovercraft Ltd. had formed Seaspeed in March 1966 and within months were operating two SRN 6 38 seater craft on the Cowes - Southampton route. Then on 23rd March 1967, a Cowes - Portsmouth link was launched using a similar SRN 6 and a special mobile pontoon at the Harbour pier.

A third route, from Portsmouth to Ryde Pier, was started on 1st April 1968 using a 65 seater Hovermarine HM 2. This was a side-walled craft driven by conventional screws whereas the SRN 6 was a cushion craft and was equally at home on land as well as water. The early service was most unreliable and all sorts of technical troubles beset it. A second such craft (numbered *002* and red-hulled) later joined the prototype and later still, on 29th September 1969 the Cowes - Portsmouth service was suspended.

By early 1970, Seaspeed were using craft *004* and *007* on the Ryde route and both were sent for modifications, re-entering service on 22nd May, *007* with *Seaspeed III* on her stern.

Meanwhile the prototype (*001*) had been refitted with Mk.III modifications and renumbered *301* entering service in January 1971. With the HM 2 craft now achieving some 85% reliability, British Rail announced that their five year plan included replacement of the diesel ships and in June 1971, an experimental call was made on weekdays at Clarence Pier but this was not repeated.

At Southampton the SRN 6 craft were proving very successful. Craft *009* and *011* were enlarged by having a 10 ft. centre section added thereby enabling them to carry 57 instead of 38 passengers. The first was named *Sea Hawk* and the second, *Sea Eagle*, the

'Hawk' re-entering service on 23rd March 1972.

The year 1972 also saw Seaspeed planning to run their successful SRN 6's on the Portsmouth - Ryde route and sharing the Hovertravel terminal adjacent to Ryde Esplanade station. The reason for this change of approach soon became clear when Seaspeed operated the summer season with just craft *004*, until 7th September when the link was closed.

The Southampton - Cowes hovercraft service closed on 1st May 1976 after which the route was taken over by Solent Seaspeed, a subsidiary of Hovertravel (operators of the Southsea - Ryde service) although the two Mk III hovercraft were owned by the British Hovercraft Corporation of East Cowes.

So ended British Rail's short flirtation with fast ferries. The services had briefly blossomed and looked good for the future but had ended in failure. However, the local management had gained

*Arriving at Ryde Pier in August 1969 is Seaspeed's first high speed craft for the route, the 65 seater HM2 **001**. (John Hendy)*

much useful experience and with the *Shanklin* withdrawn from service in March 1980, they chartered the high speed catamaran *Highland Seabird* for a week of trials during peak periods. Commuters were offered the chance of experiencing the Clyde-based vessel at no extra charge.

The *Shanklin* was sold during October 1980 to supporters of the preserved paddle steamer *Waverley*, based in Glasgow. The faulty engine was completely stripped-down and rebuilt and she emerged as the *Prince Ivanhoe* - a bargain indeed for £25,000! Spending the summer season in the Bristol Channel, luck was not on her side and on 3rd August 1981, she hit an uncharted underwater obstruction off the Gower Peninsula, was holed, beached, flooded and subsequently written-off - a tragic end for such a fine vessel.

By 1982, it was confidently expected that three Norwegian-built catamarans each carrying 500 passengers across Spithead in 10 minutes would be in service for the 1983 season. However, there was a shock in store for the operators of the route. With so much money being spent on the car ferries *St. Catherine* and the *St. Helen*, the Government decided that the fast ferries would have to await Sealink's privatisation. A token presence was made during the summer of 1983 with the charter of the Vosper Hovermarine HM 218 SES (*GH 2094*), *Ryde Rapide*. It was not a very successful season and the experiment was not repeated.

And so, the *Southsea* and the *Brading* soldiered on and were returned to private ownership in July 1984 when Sealink U.K. Ltd. was denationalised and sold to the Bermuda-based Sea Containers Ltd. Ordered by Southern Railway and launched in March 1948 as

British Railway's first new ships, they lasted for the entire nationalised era.

Plans were now announced for a 351 seater Swedish catamaran due for the 1985 season but a misunderstanding between the builders and Sealink's new owners saw the deal fall through. Now International Catamarans of Hobart, Tasmania were contacted to build a pair of craft.

Each was to cost £1.9 million and carry up to 470 passengers (later reduced to 448) across Spithead in 15 minutes. It was planned to keep the *Brading* in service until March 1986 when she would be replaced by the first of the new 'cats,' but to retain her until the end of May when the second was due to arrive. A car ferry maintained the route during overhaul periods - a usual move since the *Shanklin* 's withdrawal in March 1980 - but the *Brading* broke down and then broke down again on 21st February after which time the company decided that they could spend no more money on a ship so close to retirement.

On 17th March the first 'cat', *Our Lady Patricia*, arrived as deck cargo at Antwerp. She reached Portsmouth, via Folkestone, on the following evening and went into service on 29th March.

The second craft *Our Lady Pamela* arrived directly from Hobart under her own power on 30th July and took up service on 9th August. As from that day, the *Southsea* became the relief ship and her 38 year reign was over. High tech., high speed and high cost had won the day and the most controversial craft ever to operate to Ryde now set out to prove themselves.

The route was in severe financial trouble and the *Southsea* and *Brading* were very aged and run-down. There is no doubt that the catamarans were viewed with very mixed feelings by some of Sealink's customers, but independent market research showed that at least two out of every three passengers preferred the craft to the old diesels. The crucial factor is that the Ryde route now started to make a reasonable contribution and passenger carryings increased after many years of decline.

The remaining diesel ferry, *Southsea* was used as a cruise ship during the summers of 1987 and 1988 sailing to Sandown, Yarmouth and the Needles in her first year while Sandown calls were abandoned in favour of Southampton and Cowes in 1988. The economics of running such a large vessel in an area already flooded with smaller excursion ships proved too difficult to overcome for all those connected with the ship's operation and sadly she was withdrawn at the end of the 1988 season on 15th September. On 1st November, she would have celebrated forty years in service.

On 13th June 1989 she sailed to Falmouth for lay-up, a sad day for her many supporters. This was truly the end of an era. She had quickly built up a very loyal following during her two years of cruising although it was hoped to retain her locally in some static role as a final reminder of a classic Isle of Wight ferry.

Meanwhile, Portsmouth - Ryde was left in the hands of the twin catamarans which were given the highest seal of approval on 13th May 1987 when *Our Lady Pamela* undertook a special trip from East Cowes to Portsmouth with Her Majesty the Queen and the Duke of Edinburgh aboard. The Royal Standard flew at her mast.

Following a worldwide search for new ferries for the Ryde link,

*After her epic 13.987 mile voyage from Australia, the catamaran **Our Lady Pamela** (registered in Hobart and flying the Tasmanian flag) passes the **St. Catherine** in Spithead. (FotoFlite)*

during February 2000 it was revealed that Wightlink had purchased two 40 metre passenger catamarans from the Philippines. They were built during 1996 in Singapore by Kvaerner Fjellstrand originally being called *Waterjet 2* and then *Supercat 18* (now *FastCat-Shanklin*) and *Waterjet 1* followed by *Supercat 17* (now *FastCat-Ryde*). They were purchased from Waterjet Netherlands Antilles N.V. for $9 million and had been chartered to The Philippine Fast Ferry Company for service from Cebu. Although they would supplement rather than directly replace the

1986 pair, it was becoming evident that intensive use of the Tasmanian-built craft was requiring lengthy overhaul periods and it was therefore essential that Wightlink were able to offer their customers a reliable service without the need to charter local pleasure boats in times of need.

The first of the new 34 knot catamarans, the *FastCat-Shanklin*, arrived at Portsmouth on board the heavy lift ship *Gloria* on 12th August 2000 and was later made fast alongside the spare berth at the Gunwharf Terminal. Her sister, the *FastCat-Ryde*, arrived on the lift ship *Wilma* on 15th September. Both had their crew accommodation removed in Cebu where they were refurbished

Our Lady Patricia arriving at Portsmouth and wearing the original Wightlink livery. (John Hendy)

*The **FastCat-Shanklin** undergoing pre-service trials at Ryde Pier Head in August 2000. (John Hendy)*

and customised for Wightlink's use before entering service with a passenger capacity for 361. Due to the fact that their length prevents them from berthing starboard side to their Portsmouth Harbour berth, they unusually dock with their port side adjacent to the piers and whereas the earlier fast craft are propelled by twin propellers, the new vessels are powered by twin waterjets.

The 'Shanklin' entered service from Portsmouth to Ryde on 16th August while the 'Ryde' made her debut on 9th October. They were both officially named at a ceremony alongside the Gunwharf Terminal on 16th October.

LYMINGTON - YARMOUTH
The Western Link

Wightlink's Lymington to Yarmouth route is, in many ways, the back door to the Isle of Wight. Whereas the Portsmouth links are hustle and bustle, sailing from a great city to the "Garden Isle", the approaches to Lymington take one through the wild and beautiful New Forest before the forests of trees give way to the forests of masts in the busy yacht haven.

The delightful market town of Lymington is not the place where one would expect to find an active ferry terminal but over a million passengers a year pass through it, sailing to or returning from the equally delightful town of Yarmouth.

The route has always provided problems with navigation. On setting off to the Island, the Lymington River's deep water channel meanders in great sweeps through an extensive region of salt-marsh which culminates in Cocked-hat corner where wind and tide have caused so many groundings through the years. Today's Wightlink vessels are not only the largest ever to operate the historic route but are also the most powerful and manoeuvrable and they certainly need to be to keep to their busy and demanding schedules.

Once out of the confines of the Lymington River, in which constant comings and goings of yachtsmen of all abilities also present tremendous problems, the route to Yarmouth crosses the

*The **Solent** of 1863 and the **Mayflower** of 1866 alongside the new railway at Lymington. (Eric Payne collection)*

western Solent. Here one catches a glimpse of the distant Needles beyond which lies the grey English Channel from which the prevailing southwesterlies constantly pound the Hampshire coastline. The tidal sweeps through the narrow Solent are also extremely powerful and for lesser vessels would present serious problems when crossing the ebb and flow on this, the shortest of Wightlink's three island routes.

It was not until July 1858 that the independent Lymington Railway was opened, running down from a junction just west of Brockenhurst on the main line from London, to Lymington - a distance of some five miles.

The London and South Western Railway took control in 1879 and on 1st May 1884 extended the railway to Lymington Pier thereby allowing crossings to Yarmouth to be undertaken at all stages and states of the tide. The railway company took full control of the ferry service shortly afterwards and continued to operate the link until 1923.

It was the locally owned *Glasgow* which opened the crossing to steam navigation on 5th April 1830, having been built two years earlier at Newcastle. She measured just 53.5 ft. long with a beam of 13.5 4ft. and made the crossing in 30 minutes. These early services were extended to Cowes, Ryde and Portsmouth - the road communications in the Solent region being so poor.

For many years, cargo was shipped to the Wight in specially

*The diminutive **Lymington** of 1893 offered her passengers little in the way of shelter or comfort. (Eric Payne collection)*

constructed tow-boats which looked like half-barges with a gate across the end. These could handle livestock or goods over a slipway and were usually pulled by the steamer. The first of the tow-boats was introduced in May 1836 and proved to be a great innovation, especially as the travelling public did not have to share the decks of their ships with frightened farm animals. However, during periods of bad weather, when the tow-boats could not be pulled, passengers frequently found themselves sharing the accommodation with the odd pig or cow. Fortunately this practice has long since ceased!

The larger *Solent* came on station during the summer of 1841 having been specifically built for the route at Northam, Southampton. Her entry into service saw the *Glasgow* kept on the local ferry crossing while she maintained the longer Solent passages.

A newspaper cutting of 1842 refers to the new ship as, "the admired, new and fast iron packet steamer" which was then operating three times each week from Lymington to Yarmouth, Cowes, Ryde and Portsmouth.

By the end of the decade, the *Glasgow* had been withdrawn and in anticipation of the increased traffic which the new railway line would bring, the *Red Lion* (54 gross tons) was introduced in June 1858. The ship had been built at North Shields some two years earlier.

After twenty years of service, the first *Solent* was withdrawn during 1861 and was replaced two years later by a larger steamer of the same name. The new *Solent* (61 gross tons) was actually built locally at Lymington but was towed to Southampton for her

*With the statutory tow-boat astern, the 1902 **Solent** provided greater covered accommodation for her passengers. (Eric Payne collection)*

situated for excursionists to step straight off their trains from Bournemouth and directly onto the waiting ships.

The South Western's first ship for the passage did not appear until 1893 and was named *Lymington*. Her accommodation received much praise with the main saloon being upholstered in Utrecht velvet and the ceilings painted in white and gold. Wooden panels of maple and oak completed the effect and measuring 120 ft. by 18 ft. the ship held a passenger certificate for 311.

The *Lymington's* maiden voyage was duly completed on 9th May and another new ship, a further-named *Solent*, entered service in March 1902, having been constructed in Southampton.

The year 1913 saw 700 cars landed at Yarmouth Quay by tow-

engines to be fitted. There followed the *Mayflower*, from Newcastle, in July 1866 by which time the sailings eastwards through the Solent had been reduced to just one per week during the summer season.

As previously mentioned, the railway company bought-out the Solent Steam Packet Company in July 1884 purchasing the *Solent* and the *Mayflower* for £2,750. The *Red Lion* had been sold four years earlier.

By the time that the railway had pushed on to Lymington Pier, some of the Yarmouth services had been extended to serve Totland while the odd one even went as far as Alum Bay Pier. Cruises too had become increasingly popular, Lymington Pier being ideally

*The delightful **Freshwater** (1927) enters the Lymington River with her sail hoisted in order to aid manoeuvrability within its confines.*

barges, a rise of 400 since 1907. At this period, the Lymington route was the most popular with motorists and was far more convenient than crossing from Portsmouth to Ryde. However, in order to free the steamers for their scheduled timetables, a special tug had by this time been allocated for barge towing.

During the Great War, the service was continued although calls at Totland were severely curtailed. They were finally abandoned in 1927 although there was a time when uproar had occurred at Yarmouth following plans to call at Totland before going to call there!

The formation of the Southern Railway Company in 1923 saw continued growth and in 1927, the largest and last paddle steamer was added to the fleet. This was the delightful *Freshwater* which

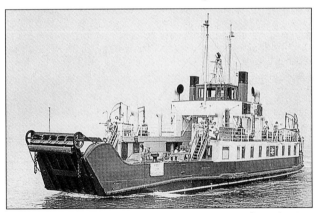

*The route's first car ferry **Lymington** arriving at Yarmouth in July 1971. (John Hendy collection)*

was built at the East Cowes yard of J. Samuel White. The new steamer boasted far greater covered accommodation for her passengers and entered service on 2nd June.

It was by this time becoming evident that the volume of motor cars was causing severe operational problems on the crossing. In 1930, vehicle numbers had risen to 1,650, this inspite of a drive on car ferry operation at Portsmouth. Even today the route attracts many people simply because it is so different and a delightful alternative to those from the west of England or from the Midlands wishing to avoid the motorway network out of London.

There was much discussion and deliberation concerning a specially constructed car ferry for Lymington which was complicated by the intervention of a new company, the Isle of Wight Ferry Co. who announced that they were to start a fresh service from Keyhaven to Fort Victoria (the closest part of the island to the mainland) using two redundant Mersey ferries following the opening of the Mersey tunnel.

The Southern Railway appeared interested in joining the new company and much to the dismay of both Yarmouth and the Isle of Wight County Council, entered into negotiations with them.

It was an interesting idea but no money was forthcoming to purchase the Mersey ferries and much time was wasted before the Southern finally announced that it was to build its own vessel.

CAR FERRIES

This was the revolutionary *Lymington* which became the first British ferry to be powered by the Voith-Schneider method of propulsion which enabled her to move in any direction without rudders. She was built at Denny's Dumbarton yard on the Clyde and was able to carry some 400 passengers and 16 cars.

The double-ended ship entered service on 1st May 1938 being scheduled to operate seven round crossings each day and becoming the year round workhorse on the passage. Inspite of some serious teething problems with the new form of propulsion, cars carried in 1938 numbered just over 4,000 compared with almost 2,500 in the previous year.

The special slipways constructed on both sides of the Solent allowed cars to drive directly on and off while during the summer peak periods, the paddle steamers *Freshwater* and *Solent* would offer an additional service from Lymington Pier to Yarmouth Pier.

During the Second World War, the *Solent* was used on the Portsmouth to Ryde link but before hostilities had ceased, a new car ferry was being planned for the western Solent.

This was the diesel electric paddle vessel *Farringford* (named after Lord Tennyson's former house in West Wight) which entered service on 4th March 1948 on delivery from Denny of Dumbarton.

The *Farringford* was the largest yet measuring 178 ft. by 50 ft. and carrying 320 passengers and 32 cars or 800 passengers without vehicles.

By 1955 the number of cars being carried had risen to 42,000 and it came as no surprise when the order for a third car ferry was made. The new *Freshwater* came from the Ailsa yard at Troon and entered service on 21st September 1959. She was not quite as large as the previous ferry and settled down to work the route with her companions - a state of affairs which existed until the end of the 1973 season. She was the last Isle of Wight ferry to be fitted with

*The diesel-electric paddle vessel **Farringford** leaving the Lymington River in July 1971. (John Hendy collection)*

deck sockets for sheep pens but it is doubtful if she ever carried any walk on - walk off livestock.

By the late sixties, improvements were put in hand to enlarge the shore facilities as cars carried in 1967 had reached 109,000. At the same time plans were announced for two new ships. The frequency of crossings was to be increased and in 1971, in order for this to be achieved, dredging in the Lymington River was completed to allow two vessels to pass each other within its confines.

Three identical sister ships were ordered from the Robb Caledon yard at Dundee - the first for the Portsmouth station and

*The **Cenwulf** is captured during a crossing to Lymington in August 1979. (John Hendy)*

the other two for Lymington. The *Cenwulf* was the first local ship and made her maiden voyage on 18th October 1973 (replacing the *Lymington*) while the *Cenred* followed in January 1974 and replaced the *Farringford* which was, in turn, sent to the Hull - New Holland service. This she continued to operate until the opening of the Humber Bridge.

The new ships could accommodate 750 passengers and 52 cars and measured 190 ft. by 51 ft. The *Freshwater* was retained as a summer back-up ferry until her own withdrawal at the end of the 1983 season.

Surprisingly, the *Lymington*, *Farringford* and *Freshwater* all eventually passed to the ownership of Western Ferries for their route across the upper Firth of Clyde although the *Farringford* was never to operate for them and was scrapped in Hull during 1984. In 1988, the *Lymington* (by then renamed the *Sound of Sanda*) celebrated her fifty years in service - an amazing record for a ferry of her type.

The larger ferries on station generated their own traffic and during their first year they shipped 179,000 cars while for the first time, a million passengers were carried.

The entry into service of the new Portsmouth car ferries *St. Catherine* and *St. Helen* during 1983 rendered the *Caedmon* surplus to local requirements and so she moved westwards to join her sisters during November.

The fitting of mezzanine decks during 1977-78, increased car capacity to 70 while the construction of Iinkspans at Lymington in 1976 and at Yarmouth in 1983 enabled speedier turn-rounds and easier embarkation for the increasing flow of heavy vehicles using the western Solent link.

*The **Cenred** leaving the Lymington River on a busy Saturday morning in August 2000. (John Hendy)*

In recent years the passenger accommodation on all three of the 'C' class has been uprated and refurbished in line with the work that had taken place on the Portsmouth-based ferries.

Plans have been drawn up and are under consideration for new ferries to operate this route but many important issues have to be considered, resulting in a long consultative and design process. The Lymington River is a very sensitive area and poses many problems of an environmental nature. Any new ships will require low draught and minimum wash characteristics and it is hoped that Wightlink will soon be in a position to introduce replacement vessels on this most attractive of island routes.

*The **Caedmon** in the Lymington River in August 1987. (John Hendy)*

ACKNOWLEDGEMENTS

As with the previous two editions of this publication I must put on record my sincere thanks and appreciation to the late Eric D.G. Payne of Ryde for leaving me his notes and cuttings relating to this trio of sea routes to the Isle of Wight. The sight of his carefully typed sheets, full of fascinating information gleaned from many hours of painstaking research on both sides of the Solent, has made my task that much easier and this book is as much his as it is mine.

For photographs, my thanks are also due to Eric Payne, George Cook, the Henry Maxwell collection, Tom Rayner and Andrew Cooke. Peter Newberry has supplied extra historical information. My daughter Alison has assisted with the typewritten manuscript and my wife Stella (born on the island and proud of it) kindly offered her services as proof reader. My business partner Miles Cowsill transferred my rough lay-out onto disk and undertook the book's design while Andrew Lowe of Haven Colourprint designed the covers.

Within Wightlink, my grateful thanks are due to: Chief Executive Michael Aiken for agreeing to write the Foreword, to Captain Dennis Ford for his considered and professional input and to the Marketing team for their interest, enthusiasm and support throughout.